Tell Me WHY

SPACE

Questions and Answers

by
Rebecca Phillips-Bartlett

Minneapolis, Minnesota

Credits
All images are courtesy of Shutterstock.com, unless otherwise specified. With thanks to Getty Images, Thinkstock Photo, iStockphoto, Adobe Stock, and NASA Image and Video Library.

Cover – BNP Design Studio, GarikProst, GoodStudio, Torontotokio, Orgus88. Throughout – BNP Design Studio, Orgus88, Natalia Sheinkin, Ali Designer 20, Nattapol_Sritongcom, Aliva, Perfectorius. 4–5 – Art Alex, janrysavy, Elen11, PhonlamaiPhoto. 6–7 – AspctStyle, Pics Garden, Ihor Biliavskyi, T. Lesia, pioneer111. 8–9 – Designer things, Nursery Art Design, NASA. 10–11 – cosmaa, Macrovector, Nick To, Artsiom P. 12–13 – Irina Strelnikova, denayunebgt, HCavid, NASA. 14–15 – ClassicVector, Colorfuel Studio, PremiumVector, Maksym Narodenko, Siraphatphoto. 16–17 – BNP Design Studio, BlueRingMedia, Elen11, NASA Images. 18–19 – Art Alex, BNP Design Studio, denayunebgt, Deagreez. 20–21 – Nevada31, Vivi Petru, castigatio. 22–23 – michaeljung, 24K-Production.

Bearport Publishing Company Product Development Team
Publisher: Jen Jenson; Director of Product Development: Spencer Brinker; Managing Editor: Allison Juda; Editor: Cole Nelson; Associate Editor: Naomi Reich; Associate Editor: Tiana Tran; Art Director: Colin O'Dea; Designer: Kim Jones; Designer: Kayla Eggert; Product Development Specialist: Owen Hamlin

Library of Congress Cataloging-in-Publication Data is available at www.loc.gov or upon request from the publisher.

ISBN: 979-8-89232-756-5 (hardcover)
ISBN: 979-8-89232-952-1 (paperback)
ISBN: 979-8-89232-843-2 (ebook)

© 2025 BookLife Publishing
This edition is published by arrangement with BookLife Publishing.

North American adaptations © 2025 Bearport Publishing Company. All rights reserved. No part of this publication may be reproduced in whole or in part, stored in any retrieval system, or transmitted in any form or by any means, electronic, mechanical, photocopying, recording, or otherwise, without written permission from the publisher.

For more information, write to Bearport Publishing, 5357 Penn Avenue South, Minneapolis, MN 55419.

Contents

Tell Me Why 4
Why Do Stars Twinkle? 6
Why Can't I See Stars during the Day? 7
Why Do People Live in Space? 8
Why Haven't We Found Aliens? 9
Why Haven't We Visited Mars? 10
Why Do Things Float in the International
   Space Station? 12
Why Do Astronauts Wear Spacesuits? 14
Why Do Astronauts Eat Special Food? 15
Why Do Some Planets Have Rings? 16
Why Can't I Feel Earth Move? 17
Why Do We Have Leap Years? 18
Why Does the Moon Change Shape? 20
Why Do We Have Meteor Showers? 21
Asking Questions 22
Glossary 24
Index 24

TELL ME WHY

Throughout history, people have been curious about what is in space. From the planets in our solar system to the stars beyond, there is so much to learn about space.

Space is huge. Sometimes, the things we notice about it seem very strange. This can leave us wondering **WHY?**

QUESTION
What questions do you have about space?

WHY DO STARS TWINKLE?

If you look up at the night sky, you may notice that the stars twinkle. However, stars actually shine at a steady brightness. They only appear to twinkle because of Earth's **atmosphere**.

By the time a star's light reaches Earth, it has been bent many times as it passed through the atmosphere. This movement makes it look like the star is twinkling.

WHY CAN'T I SEE STARS DURING THE DAY?

The stars we see at night are very far away, and their light is faint when it reaches Earth. Our sun is a star close to Earth. So, its light is very bright.

During the day, the stars are still in the sky. But the sun makes the sky so bright that you can't see the other stars.

WHY DO PEOPLE LIVE IN SPACE?

About 250 miles (400 km) above Earth, **astronauts** live in a spacecraft called the International Space Station (ISS). They are there to do important **research** that can't be done anywhere else. Scientists on the ISS do lots of things, including studying how space affects the human body.

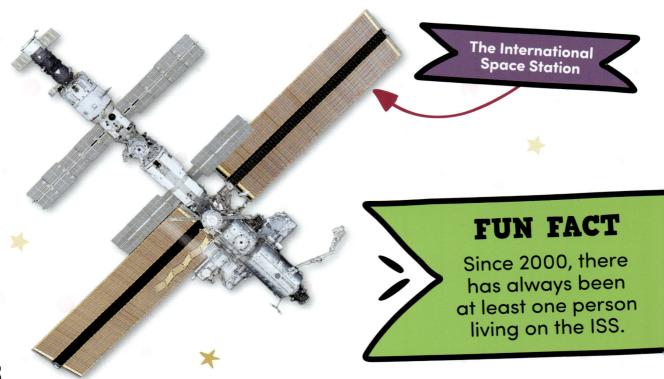

The International Space Station

FUN FACT

Since 2000, there has always been at least one person living on the ISS.

WHY HAVEN'T WE FOUND ALIENS?

QUESTION
Do you think there is alien life somewhere in space?

The word *alien* means life that comes from another planet.

Some people believe our **universe** could be home to alien life. However, they think our **technology** isn't advanced enough to find it yet. The tools scientists use to search space, such as spacecraft, have limited ranges. This makes it difficult to search for signs of life on distant planets.

WHY HAVEN'T WE VISITED MARS?

Although Mars is the closest planet to Earth, it is still very far away. Because of this distance, spacecraft would need a lot of **fuel** just to get to Mars. This amount of fuel would be very heavy and would take up too much room on a spacecraft.

FUN FACT
We have sent **remote-controlled** robots called rovers to explore Mars.

The distance would be a problem for the astronaut crew, too. Being in space too long can be **dangerous** to the human body. Scientists are studying astronauts on the ISS to find an answer to this problem.

WHY DO THINGS FLOAT IN THE INTERNATIONAL SPACE STATION?

Gravity pulls everything on Earth toward the ground. It also acts on astronauts in space. The ISS and everything on it are falling toward Earth due to gravity. But that is not the only direction they are moving.

FUN FACT
Gravity pulls all objects toward one another. Larger objects have a stronger pull.

The ISS and everything on it are also going around the planet, as though moving forward. This happens at about the same speed as the tug down. Because of this, the forces equal out. Astronauts on the ship are not pulled in any one direction. They float.

FUN FACT
When two forces pull against something equally, they balance each other out.

WHY DO ASTRONAUTS WEAR SPACESUITS?

When astronauts leave their spacecraft, they need protection. Spacesuits keep them safe from some of the dangers in space, including dust and very bright sunlight. These special suits provide astronauts with air to breathe and water to drink. Spacesuits also help control the astronauts' body **temperature**.

WHY DO ASTRONAUTS EAT SPECIAL FOOD?

Imagine trying to eat a meal while your food keeps floating off your plate. This can happen to astronauts. So, the space explorers eat special foods. Space food must be carefully packaged to last a long time and so it doesn't make a mess. It is often served in cans or plastic pouches.

FUN FACT
Bread is not allowed in spacecraft because it creates crumbs that can damage equipment!

WHY DO SOME PLANETS HAVE RINGS?

Some planets are surrounded by rings made of rock, ice, and dust. Scientists have a few ideas about why this happens.

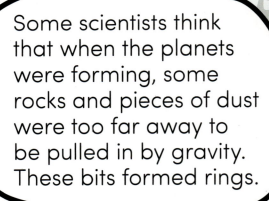

Some scientists think that when the planets were forming, some rocks and pieces of dust were too far away to be pulled in by gravity. These bits formed rings.

Others believe the planets had moons that crashed together and broke apart. The remains formed rings.

WHY CAN'T I FEEL EARTH MOVE?

Earth is always moving. It moves in a path around the sun, and it also spins. However, you feel movement only when there is a change in speed. Neither of Earth's movements speed up or slow down. Because of this, you don't feel Earth move.

WHY DO WE HAVE LEAP YEARS?

The length of a year is how long it takes a planet to go around the sun.

Our standard year has 365 days. However, it actually takes Earth about 365 and one quarter days to complete its **orbit**.

To keep our calendars matched up with Earth's journey around the sun, every four years we have a year with 366 days. This is called a leap year. In a leap year, February has 29 days instead of its usual 28.

FUN FACT
People who are born on February 29th have their actual birthday once every four years!

WHY DOES THE MOON CHANGE SHAPE?

The moon doesn't make its own light. Instead, its surface **reflects** light from the sun. As the moon travels around Earth in its orbit, we only see the sun's light on parts of it. This makes the moon look as though it changes shape in the sky.

FUN FACT
The different shapes of the moon are known as moon phases.

WHY DO WE HAVE METEOR SHOWERS?

When bits of rock, ice, and dust enter Earth's atmosphere, they are called meteors. Most meteors burn up and create bright lines of light in the sky. A meteor shower is when there are many meteors at the same time. This can happen when Earth moves through a cloud of space dust and rock.

Asking Questions

Asking questions is a great way to learn more about the universe. Just like you, scientists have a lot of questions about space.

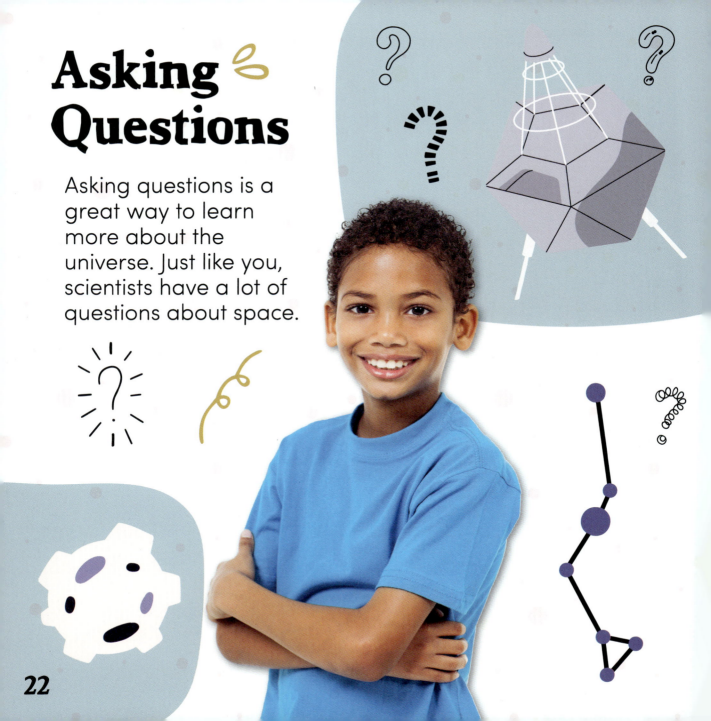

There is still plenty to discover about everything in space. So, stay curious, and keep asking questions!

QUESTION
What other questions do you have about space?

Glossary

astronauts people who travel into space

atmosphere the layer of gases that make up the air that surrounds a planet

dangerous likely to cause harm or injury

fuel something that is burned to produce heat or power

gravity a strong force that pulls objects toward one another

orbit the curved path that objects travel in while going around planets or stars

reflects bounces back light, heat, or sound

remote-controlled operated by a device from a distance

research information collected through experiments or studies

technology useful things made to do work or solve a problem

temperature how hot or cold something is

universe the planets, moons, stars, and everything else in space

Index

aliens 9
astronauts 8, 11, 14–15
bodies 8, 11, 14
foods 15
gravity 12–13, 16
moons 4, 16, 20
orbit 18, 20
rocks 16, 21
spacecraft 8–9, 14–15
stars 4, 6–7
sun 4, 7, 14, 17–20
years 18–19